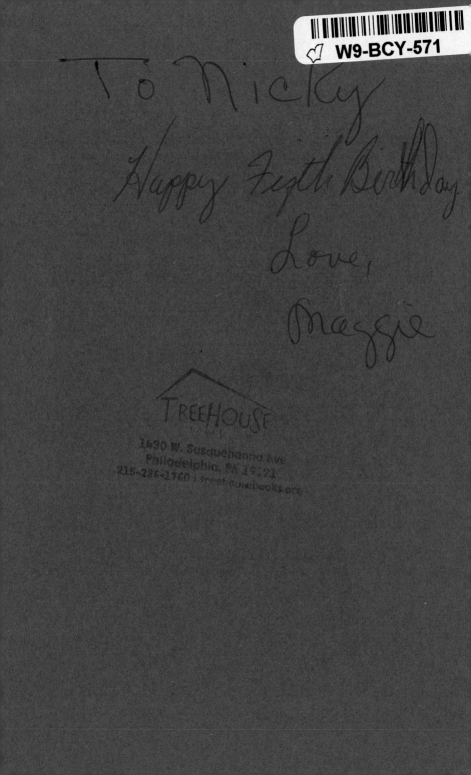

W9-BCY-571

To Nicky

Happy Fifth Birthday

Love,

Maggie

Wonder Why

RUTH HARNDEN

 Illustrated by
Elaine Livermore

Houghton Mifflin Company Boston 1971

LIBRARY OF CONGRESS CATALOG CARD NUMBER 78-161652
ISBN 0-395-12755-6   ISBN 0-395-12756-4 DOL.
PRINTED IN THE UNITED STATES OF AMERICA
FIRST PRINTING   H

For Sylvia

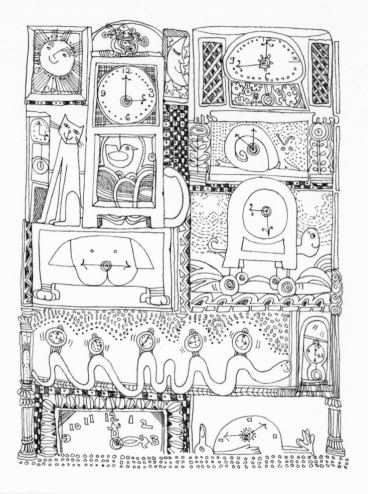

1

Time doesn't listen to anyone
And behaves in the oddest way,
Sometimes fast and sometimes slow,
All on the very same day.

It seems to do the opposite
Of what would be my way;
It crawls when I want it to hurry,
And runs when I want it to stay.

If I could really tell the time
I'd have two things to say:
I'd tell it to race when I'm at school,
And creep when I'm out to play.

2 I often break a glass or dish,
No matter how I try,
But my cat is far more graceful,
And cleverer than I.

He likes the china closet
And goes in there for fun.
He walks amongst the tumblers
And never tumbles one.

He has four feet to think of
And also a tail behind,
And yet he seems to keep them
All carefully in mind.

My dog is much more clumsy
And things fall down and break
When he's around to wave his tail
Or give himself a shake.

I love them both and they love me,
And yet I wonder whether
My cat hasn't got more sense than both
My dog and me together.

3

Why does it have to be my fate
To continually wait?

I wait for the bus to take me to school,
Then I wait to get home again as a rule.
I wait for lunch and I wait for dinner
While I get hungrier and thinner.
I wait for my mother to market and shop,
And nothing I say makes her hurry or stop.
But no one ever says "Just wait,"
And lets me go to bed more late.
Waiting is about the first
Of all the things that I hate worst.

Why aren't grownups made to be
Anywhere near as patient as me?

4   I'm supposed to like the baby
Who's supposed to be my brother,
Though all he does is eat and sleep
And monopolize my mother.

She says I can't be selfish,
But as far as I can see
The baby is more selfish
Than two or three of me.

He doesn't even try to please,
To mind or be polite,
But spits his food, and makes a mess,
And sometimes cries all night.

If I do things not half as bad,
And lots of things just right,
They either scold, or make me feel
That he is far more bright.

No matter what they tell me
About loving me and stuff,
If they really loved me,
Why wasn't I enough?

And how would they be apt to feel
If I came home someday
With a brand-new second mother
Who moved right in to stay?

5

There are so many kinds of birds
And animals and fish,
And as different trees and flowers
As anyone could wish.
It seems to me that God must be
Specially fond of variety.

With people, too, all shades and sizes,
And talking differently,
It should be very clear to see
It's part of God's variety
For everyone to be unique
In how they look, and think, and speak.

6

If I were bigger than anyone,
If I were taller than trees,
I could step over hills and towns
And go anywhere I please.

I could be everywhere at once
If I were part of the sky,
And no one could make me heed or hear
However they might try.

No one could order me about,
Or scold or criticize —
That is, if I should make myself
A hundred times their size.

But I might choose to be instead
So very, very small
That I would not be visible
To anyone at all.

I'd hide in people's pockets,
Or burrow in their hair,
And none of them would ever know
That I was even there.

If I got bored with being huge,
The next day I'd be small.
But the size I really am
I might not choose at all.

7

I had a bear in my closet.
He came when the light was out.
So of course I couldn't see him,
But still I hadn't a doubt.
I heard him pushing shoes and things
Along the closet floor.
He made a fearful racket
Clawing at the door.
I didn't dare to move,
And I didn't like to scream,
And so I tried to tell myself
I was having a bad dream.

But I was wide awake,
And I was sure of that
When I heard the hunting voice
Of my big tiger cat.
My cat's as brave as a tiger,
Besides, he can see at night.
He made me feel quite silly,
But very safe and nice,
By chasing the bear
I thought was there —
Who was really a couple of mice.

8 Mister Jeremy Appleby Briggs
Is old, as you might suppose,
But he started out by being young
As anyone sensible knows.

He must have run and climbed and swung
And made a lot of noise,
And doubtless was as mischievous
As all the other boys.

But now he goes as carefully
Along the village street,
As though to simply walk at all
Were something of a feat.

His neighbors say, "Good morning, Sir."
And "How are you today?"
But I've never heard him answer
In a happy sort of way.

And what I sometimes wonder is —
Has he quite forgot?
Or if I tossed my ball to him
Mightn't it be caught?

9

Some things I want to have different and new,
Like clothes, or a book, or a game,
But when it comes to what I eat
I want it always the same.

I know exactly what I like,
And it agrees with me,
So I can eat it every day
Very contentedly.

Nothing's wrong with my appetite.
In fact, if you ask me,
People who want all different meals
Aren't hungry as they should be.

Or maybe they keep on hoping
They'll sometime find a treat
That they like just as much as I
Like what I always eat.

10

I had a cat this morning,
And I had a cat last night,
But somehow today
Along the way
He's got himself lost from sight.

He isn't in the attic,
Nor down the cellar stairs.
The closets are bare
Of even a hair,
And so are his favorite chairs.

I've searched behind the book shelves
And I've looked beneath the beds.
I know that he's bound
To be somewhere around,
If I knew where a hiding cat heads.

Someone always finds me,
Though I never make a sound,
So probably he
Is smarter than me —
Or maybe I want to be found.

11   Why does space become so big
When it has no light,
And then get small and safe again
As soon as it is bright?

My room is just my size
And I know it very well,
Bed and chair and bureau,
Door and windowsill.

By morning it returns,
So I know it's really here,
But when my light's turned out
It seems to disappear.

There isn't any bureau,
There isn't any door,
There isn't any ceiling —
I'm not sure there's any floor.

I wish I were a cat or dog,
So I could see at night,
And then I wouldn't feel all lost
When all I've lost is light.

12

At times I find it hard to know
What I dreamed and what is so.
I can make the same mistake
Even when I am awake.
Then things really seem to be
Exactly what I'd like to see.
But other times it's what I fear
That gets quite real, and awfully near.
If they are all in my own mind,
Why can't I choose what I want to find?

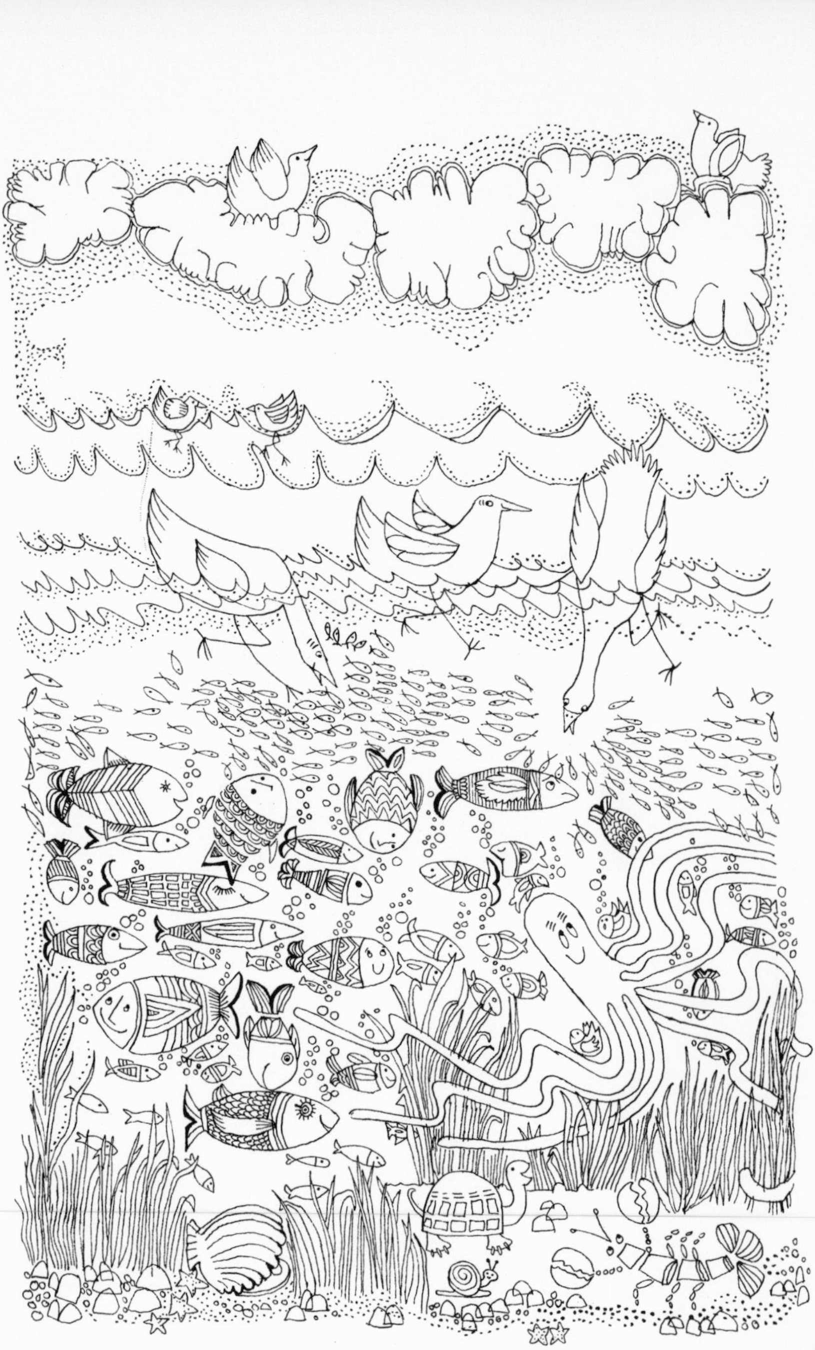

13

It's slightly hard to understand
Why people have to live on land
When both the oceans and the sky
Are much more wide or much more high
With lots more room for you and I.
And why it is the birds and fish
Have all the space that you could wish.

14

Whenever the stars are out of sight
And the night is very still,
Then I hear the foghorn blow
From the harbor down the hill.

It's calling to the baffled ships
That cannot see their way,
And trying to make sure they're safe
Until the break of day.

Snuggled safely in my bed,
Secure on my home ground,
Why do I like so much to hear
That very lonely sound?

15   When the sky turns black with night
It's very hard to trust
That daylight will come back again,
Although I know it must.

When the sun returns once more
And the sky is light,
Again it's very hard to think
I'll ever see the night.

The seasons, too, bewilder me
And I scarcely can believe
The earth will turn to growing green
And all the snow will leave.

Or when it's green and warm again
I hardly can remember
How cold and white and frozen
The world was in December.

Since people are supposed to be
In charge of everything,
How come the birds know when to go
Where it is warm as spring?

16

There once was a cat who lived on a boat.
He lived all his life completely afloat.
He couldn't chase a chipmunk, he couldn't catch a bird,
Of trees and bees and butterflies he had scarcely heard.
The world was mostly water as far as he could tell,
And water isn't something that cats like very well.

But though they dislike water they are curiously fond
Of the fish who live within it, river, sea or pond.
And so this landless cat was remarkably content
In that life for which he wasn't originally meant.

17 A beach is sometimes narrow,
    And it's sometimes very wide
    And strewn with lots of treasures
    Left by the leaving tide.

    What makes such pretty, fluted shells
    In such variety?
    Who decorated sand dollars
    In perfect symmetry?

Hundreds of sandpipers fly
As if they were just one,
And just like one they wheel and turn
To silver in the sun.

Everything about a beach
Is full of mystery,
Especially where the water goes
When the tide goes out to sea.

18

Summer, winter, spring, and fall
Where I live we have them all.
But there are places, as I know,
Where there is only snow.
Or across the world, they say,
Summer never goes away.
If I had to choose just one,
I wonder which would be more fun?

19

A farm is where I'd like to live
With a roomy barn and shed
For every homeless cat who needs
A roof above his head.

There would be some cows and horses,
Hens and chickens, too.
And every spring there'd be a calf,
And perhaps a colt or two.

No one would be hungry,
And they would all be friends,
For it's a happy dream I have
And that is how it ends.

20

Over the pasture wall the sheep
Stand in the moonlight half-asleep.
The dog who herds them guards us, too,
Faithfully the whole night through.

Soft are the feet that fall on the land
Where mist is abroad, and quiet the stand
Of one awake with the world asleep
And he in the moonlight watching sheep.